# The
# Tabernacle

Brandon M. Crooker

**The Tabernacle**

Brandon M. Crooker

Scripture quotations are from the King James Version of the Bible.

ISBN 978-1-961482-21-0

# Table of Contents

# Foreword

The Tabernacle of the Old Testament was far more than an ancient structure in the wilderness—it was a divine blueprint pointing forward to Jesus Christ. In The Tabernacle, readers are guided through a rich exploration of this sacred tent of meeting, uncovering its spiritual significance, intricate design, and powerful symbolism.

From the outer court to the Holy of Holies, every piece of furniture, every ritual, and every measurement reveals a deeper truth about God's plan of redemption. This book not only explains the historical and theological meaning behind the Tabernacle but also draws clear and compelling connections between its elements and the life, ministry, and sacrifice of Jesus Christ.

Whether you're a student of Scripture, a pastor, or simply a believer seeking a deeper appreciation of the Bible's unity, The Tabernacle will open your eyes to the foreshadowing of Christ woven throughout the pages of the Old Testament. Discover how the Tabernacle served as a prophetic pattern—a shadow of the heavenly reality and the coming Messiah.

Thoughtful, biblical, and Christ-centered, this study will deepen your understanding of God's presence, holiness, and His desire to dwell among His people.

# Introduction

When I first began to study the Tabernacle, I never could have imagined the depth of insight, beauty, and spiritual truth I would discover along the way. What started as a simple desire to better understand a portion of Scripture soon became a journey that stirred my heart, enriched my faith, and drew me closer to the God who so graciously chose to dwell among His people.

My inspiration for writing this book was sparked in part by the study and prayer pattern taught by the late G.A. Mangun. His deep reverence for God's presence and his practical guidance on praying through the Tabernacle stirred something in my spirit. As I listened and reflected on his teaching, I felt compelled not to stop at appreciation alone, but to study it out for myself. I wanted to trace the sacred pattern, piece by piece, and uncover the treasures hidden within the fabric, furnishings, and design of the Tabernacle.

The fruit of that study is what you now hold in your hands. This book is not intended as an academic treatise or a technical manual on Old Testament architecture. Rather, it is a devotional journey — an exploration of how God's ancient dwelling place in the wilderness points us to Christ, to His church, and to the ongoing work of the Holy Spirit in our lives today.

In these pages, I have tried to capture the wonder I experienced as I studied, prayed, and meditated on the Tabernacle. My hope is that you, too, will see the Tabernacle not as a relic of Israel's past, but as a living pattern that invites us into deeper fellowship with our holy God. May it inspire you, as it has inspired me, to seek His presence, to walk in His ways, and to worship according to the pattern He has revealed.

It is my prayer that as you read, the Lord will open your eyes to behold wondrous things out of His law (Psalm 119:18), and that you will find yourself drawn ever closer to the God who still desires to dwell among His people — and within their hearts.

# Chapter 1

# God's Desire to Dwell Among His People

From the very beginning of creation, we see a God who longs to dwell with His people. In the Garden of Eden, the Lord walked in the cool of the day with Adam and Eve (Genesis 3:8). His presence was not distant or hidden — it was near, intimate, and tangible. When sin entered the world, that unbroken fellowship was fractured. Yet, even in humanity's fall, the heart of God remained the same: He desired to dwell among His people.

Centuries later, on Mount Sinai, God revealed His plan to restore His presence to His chosen nation. In Exodus 25:8, God instructed Moses, "And let them make Me a sanctuary, that I may dwell among them." This was not simply a structure or a religious monument; it was the visible sign of an invisible reality — God coming to dwell with His people once again.

### The Tabernacle: A Divine Invitation

The Tabernacle, or Mishkan in Hebrew, means "dwelling place" or "residence." It was God's chosen method to make His holy presence manifest among a sinful people. This was no human invention. Every detail, measurement, and material was given by divine revelation. As Hebrews 8:5 tells us, it was "a copy and shadow of what is in heaven."

When God commanded Moses to build the Tabernacle, He was offering Israel an invitation — to come close, to worship, and to experience His glory in a tangible way. The Tabernacle was not merely about ritual; it was about relationship. It was God's way of saying: "I want to be with you. I want you to know Me."

### The Pattern Shown on the Mountain

God's instructions were precise: "According to all that I show you, that is, the pattern of the tabernacle and the pattern of all its furnishings, just so you shall make it" (Exodus 25:9). This was not the time for human creativity or innovation. The pattern was sacred because it reflected eternal truths.

Every piece of the Tabernacle — from the outer court to the Holy of Holies — symbolized a step in drawing nearer to God. Each furnishing, each fabric, each measurement revealed something of God's nature and His plan for redemption. The Tabernacle was a sermon in wood, gold, linen, and blood.

## God's Presence Among a Pilgrim People

Why did God choose a tent? The Tabernacle was portable. It moved with Israel on their journey through the wilderness. This teaches us a powerful lesson: God journeys with His people. He is not confined to a place. His desire is to be near us in every season of life — in the wilderness and in the promised land, in times of wandering and in times of settlement.

The cloud by day and the fire by night that rested above the Tabernacle reminded Israel daily that their God was near. His presence was their protection, their guide, and their glory.

## A Picture of Christ

The Tabernacle points beyond itself. Every element, from the gate of the court to the veil of the Most Holy Place, points to Jesus Christ. John 1:14 says, "And the Word became flesh and dwelt among us." The word dwelt in Greek literally means tabernacled. Jesus is the true and better Tabernacle — the living presence of God among men.

Through Christ, the barriers of sin are torn down. The veil is rent. The way into the Holy of Holies is opened, not with the blood of bulls and goats, but with His own precious blood.

## Reflection

God's desire has always been to dwell with His people. The Tabernacle shows us the lengths He goes to make that possible. It is a call to us today: Will we draw near? Will we welcome His presence?

## Key Takeaway

The Tabernacle is God's invitation to relationship, a visible sign of His invisible presence, and a prophetic picture of Christ who makes access to God possible.

# Chapter 2

# The Pattern Shown on the Mount

When God called Moses to ascend Mount Sinai, He did not merely give him commandments for moral living or civil governance. God revealed something far greater — the pattern of His dwelling place. In Exodus 25:40, the Lord instructed Moses:

"And see to it that you make them according to the pattern which was shown you on the mountain."

The Tabernacle was not a product of human imagination or ingenuity. It was a heavenly design, a copy of something real and eternal, a reflection of God's dwelling in heaven. To disregard or alter the pattern would have been to distort divine truth.

## The Sacredness of the Pattern

God is a God of order. His instructions for the Tabernacle were detailed and exact because the structure itself was a teaching tool — a revelation of God's holiness, His grace, and His plan for redemption. Every board, curtain, socket, and vessel had purpose and meaning.

Consider Hebrews 8:5, where the writer reminds us that the earthly Tabernacle served "as the copy and shadow of the heavenly things." Moses was privileged to glimpse this reality on the mount, and what he saw had to be followed precisely.

Deviation from the pattern would not just be disobedience — it would be misrepresentation. The Tabernacle was not about artistic expression; it was about divine revelation.

## The Weight of Obedience

Imagine Moses descending the mountain, his heart full of awe and wonder. In his mind's eye, he had seen heaven's pattern. His task was to faithfully replicate what had been revealed. There was no room for personal interpretation or innovation. God had spoken, and Moses was to obey.

Obedience in building the Tabernacle speaks to us today. We are called to worship and serve according to God's revealed Word, not according to our preferences or the culture around us. The Tabernacle reminds us that God defines how we approach Him. We cannot draw near on our own terms.

## The Tabernacle and the Church

Just as the Tabernacle was built according to the heavenly pattern, so the church — the Body of Christ — is to reflect God's design. Ephesians 2:21-22 describes believers as being "fitly framed together" and "built together for a habitation of God through the Spirit."

God's church is not a human institution. It is a divine construction, meant to display His glory and house His presence. The same attention to divine order and pattern that guided the building of the Tabernacle should guide how we function as His people today.

## The Shadow of the True

It is important to remember that the earthly Tabernacle was always pointing to something greater. The pattern on the mount was not just for Moses' generation — it was a prophecy in fabric, wood, and gold. It was a shadow of Christ, the true dwelling of God among men.

Colossians 2:17 tells us that such things "are a shadow of things to come, but the substance is of Christ." When we study the Tabernacle, we are not just looking at an ancient tent — we are seeing glimpses of Jesus, the fulfillment of God's plan to dwell with us forever.

## Reflection

The pattern shown to Moses teaches us to approach God with reverence and obedience. We are not free to redefine worship, holiness, or truth. Instead, we are called to follow the pattern — revealed in His Word, fulfilled in His Son, and empowered by His Spirit.

## Key Takeaway

The Tabernacle teaches that worship and access to God must follow His revealed pattern. True fellowship with God is found when we honor His design.

# Chapter 3

# The Outer Court A Place of Access

The journey into the Tabernacle began not in the Most Holy Place, nor even in the Holy Place, but in the Outer Court — a space of initial approach. This was the place where God first allowed His people to draw near. Before one could experience the glory of God's presence behind the veil, they had to come through the prescribed entrance and engage with what stood in the courtyard.

The Outer Court teaches us foundational truths about salvation, cleansing, and access to God. It reminds us that while God desires to dwell with us, we must come by His appointed way.

## The Gate: The Only Entrance

There was only one gate to the Tabernacle's courtyard (Exodus 27:16). This gate, covered in richly embroidered linen of blue, purple, and scarlet thread, symbolized the single way of access to God. It faced east, catching the first light of dawn — a symbol of hope and new beginnings.

Jesus said in John 10:9: "I am the door: by me if any man enter in, he shall be saved, and shall go in and out, and find pasture." The gate of the Tabernacle pointed forward to Christ, the only way to God. There are not many paths to the Father — only one, through the Son.

The exclusivity of the gate speaks to the exclusivity of salvation. We do not enter God's presence on our own terms, by our own merit, or through any other means but Jesus.

## The Brazen Altar: A Place of Sacrifice

The first thing seen upon entering the court was the Brazen Altar (Exodus 27:1-8). Made of acacia wood and overlaid with bronze, this altar was the site of burnt offerings, sin offerings, peace offerings, and more. It was the place of bloodshed — a stark reminder that without the shedding of blood, there is no remission of sins (Hebrews 9:22).

Every sacrifice offered on the altar pointed to the ultimate sacrifice of Jesus Christ. The fire on the altar burned continually, symbolizing God's continual readiness to receive atonement for sin.

The Brazen Altar teaches that forgiveness and fellowship with God come at a cost — the cost of life. It confronts us with the reality of sin and the necessity of substitutionary sacrifice. It is at the altar that we begin our journey toward God's presence, humbled and grateful for His provision of a Savior.

## The Laver: A Place of Cleansing

After the altar stood the Bronze Laver (Exodus 30:17-21). Made from the polished mirrors of the Israelite women, it was a basin for washing. The priests were required to wash their hands and feet before ministering at the altar or entering the Holy Place. Failure to do so meant death.

The laver signifies purification. While the altar dealt with sin's penalty, the laver addressed sin's pollution. It speaks of sanctification, the ongoing work of cleansing that prepares us to serve and enter deeper into God's presence.

For the believer today, the laver represents the washing of water by the Word (Ephesians 5:26) and the continual work of the Holy Spirit in sanctifying our lives. Just as the priests could see their reflection in the laver's polished bronze, so we see ourselves truly when we look into the mirror of God's Word.

## A Journey Begins

The Outer Court was not the end goal; it was the beginning of a journey deeper into communion with God. But it was essential. No one could bypass the altar or the laver and expect to enter the Holy Place. These elements established the foundation: sin must be dealt with, and the heart must be made clean.

Today, we are invited to the same journey. We come to the altar — to the cross of Christ — where the penalty of sin was paid. We come to the laver — to the Word and the Spirit — where we are made clean. And from there, we proceed toward ever-deeper fellowship with our God.

## Reflection

The Outer Court calls us to examine our approach to God. We are reminded that access to His presence begins at the altar of sacrifice and the laver of cleansing. We cannot come to God apart from Christ's atonement, and we cannot bypass the need for daily sanctification.

As you consider your own walk with God:

- Have you entered through the one true gate — Jesus Christ?

- Are you living in the light of His perfect sacrifice, daily remembering the price He paid for your sin?

- Are you allowing His Word and Spirit to cleanse and sanctify you as you draw nearer to Him?

The Outer Court invites us to start the journey — a journey of surrender, cleansing, and preparation for deeper intimacy with the Lord.

## Key Takeaway

The Outer Court reveals the beginning of our approach to God: through the one gate (Christ), by the blood of sacrifice (His atonement), and through cleansing (sanctification). There is no access to God without these foundations.

# Chapter 4

# The Holy Place — The Life of Devotion

Beyond the Outer Court lay the Holy Place — the first of the two sacred inner chambers of the Tabernacle. This space was set apart, reserved for the priests who ministered daily before the Lord. It was a place of sustained worship, continual service, and deeper communion. The Holy Place speaks to us of a life of devotion — a life that goes beyond initial salvation and cleansing to abiding fellowship with God.

As believers, we are invited not to linger only at the altar and laver, but to step further in — to live daily in the Holy Place, where the light, provision, and intercession of God sustain us.

### The Table of Showbread — Fellowship and Provision

On the north side of the Holy Place stood the Table of Showbread (Exodus 25:23-30). This small table, overlaid with pure gold, held twelve loaves of bread — one for each tribe of Israel. The bread was called the Bread of the Presence because it was continually set before the Lord.

The Table of Showbread teaches us of God's provision and fellowship. It speaks of Christ, the Bread of Life (John 6:35), who satisfies the deepest hunger of our souls. It also reminds us that God desires communion with His people — a shared table, a continual feast in His presence.

For the believer, this table invites us to daily fellowship with Christ, partaking of His life and relying on His provision.

### The Golden Lampstand — Light and Illumination

Opposite the table, on the south side of the Holy Place, stood the Golden Lampstand (Exodus 25:31-40). Fashioned from a single piece of beaten gold, it held seven branches with oil-filled lamps that burned continually, casting light within the otherwise dark chamber.

The lampstand symbolizes the illumination of the Holy Spirit. Just as the lampstand gave light to the Holy Place, so the Spirit gives light to our hearts, enabling us to see and understand the truths of God (John 16:13). It points us to Jesus, the Light of the World (John 8:12).

The continual flame of the lampstand challenges us to maintain the oil of the Spirit in our lives, to live in the light, and to let that light shine for the glory of God.

## The Altar of Incense — Prayer and Intercession

Directly before the veil that separated the Holy Place from the Most Holy Place stood the Altar of Incense (Exodus 30:1-10). On this small golden altar, fragrant incense was burned morning and evening, symbolizing the prayers of God's people ascending continually before Him (Psalm 141:2; Revelation 5:8).

The Altar of Incense teaches us about prayer — persistent, sweet, and pleasing to God. It reminds us that as we draw near in worship, prayer is to be constant, not occasional. The incense rising toward the veil points to Christ, our great Intercessor (Hebrews 7:25), who ever lives to make intercession for us.

For the believer, the Altar of Incense calls us to a life marked by prayer — a continual offering of our hearts and voices to the Lord.

## Living in the Holy Place

The Holy Place represents a life of sustained devotion, beyond the initial steps of salvation and cleansing. Here, the believer walks daily in fellowship (showbread), illumination (lampstand), and intercession (altar of incense).

It is in the Holy Place that we are nourished by Christ, guided by His Spirit, and drawn deeper through prayer. The Holy Place is not a destination for the elite; it is the daily calling of every believer who desires intimacy with God.

## Reflection

The Holy Place invites us into a deeper life — a life of devotion, sustained by Christ, enlightened by the Spirit, and filled with prayer.

- Are you daily feeding on the Bread of Life?
- Are you walking in the light of the Spirit?

- Are your prayers rising like incense before the throne of God?

God calls us beyond the outer courts — into His house, His presence, His heart.

## Key Takeaway

The Holy Place represents the life of the devoted believer: a life of constant fellowship, Spirit-led guidance, and unceasing prayer.

# Chapter 5

# The Veil — Separation and Invitation

As one stood within the Holy Place, the path forward was blocked by a great curtain: the veil. This veil was not just another drapery or decoration; it was a powerful symbol, rich in meaning. It marked the boundary between the Holy Place and the Most Holy Place — between where man could minister and where God's manifest glory dwelt.

The veil represents both separation because of sin, and invitation through grace. It teaches us about God's holiness, man's condition, and Christ's provision.

## The Description of the Veil

The veil was made of fine linen woven with blue, purple, and scarlet threads, embroidered with figures of cherubim (Exodus 26:31-33). It hung upon four gold-covered pillars, secured in silver sockets, and it hid the Ark of the Covenant and the Mercy Seat from view.

The colors and designs spoke volumes:

- Blue: heaven and divinity

- Purple: royalty and kingly authority

- Scarlet: sacrifice and atonement

- Cherubim: the guardians of God's holy presence

The veil communicated that access to God was not casual or assumed. The way into His presence was blocked — a barrier because of human sin.

## The Veil as Separation

The veil's presence taught Israel that God is holy and man is sinful. Though the priests could enter the Holy Place daily, only the High Priest could pass beyond the veil — and then only once a year, on the Day of Atonement (Yom Kippur). Even then, he could not enter without blood (Leviticus 16:2, 15-16).

The veil declared: "Thus far, and no farther." The people could approach God through sacrifice and prayer, but direct access was denied. The veil was both a protection and a proclamation — guarding sinful man from the consuming holiness of God.

## The Veil Torn — Christ Opens the Way

The most powerful moment in the veil's history came at the death of Jesus Christ. As He cried out and gave up His spirit, the Gospels record:

"Then, behold, the veil of the temple was torn in two from top to bottom; and the earth quaked, and the rocks were split" (Matthew 27:51).

This tearing was no human act — it was God's own hand, ripping apart the barrier that sin had raised. The death of Jesus accomplished what no sacrifice of bulls or goats could: it opened the way for all who believe to enter the very presence of God.

The torn veil declares:

- The price of sin has been paid.
- The barrier of separation is removed.
- The invitation to draw near is given.

Through Christ, we have boldness to enter the Holiest (Hebrews 10:19-20).

## The Invitation Today

Though the veil once stood as a symbol of separation, today it serves as a reminder of invitation. The writer of Hebrews urges us:

"Let us therefore come boldly to the throne of grace, that we may obtain mercy and find grace to help in time of need" (Hebrews 4:16).

The way is open. The price is paid. The presence of God is accessible — not through our merit, but through the finished work of Christ.

## Reflection

The veil teaches us both the seriousness of sin and the marvel of grace.

- Do you recognize the holiness of God and the weight of what Christ has done to grant you access?

- Are you drawing near daily to the presence of God through the new and living way Jesus opened?

Let us not take lightly the privilege of approaching God's throne. Let us come with reverence, gratitude, and faith.

## Key Takeaway

The veil represents the barrier sin created — and the invitation Christ secured. Because of Jesus, we can boldly enter God's presence.

# Chapter 6

# The Most Holy Place —
# The Presence of God

Beyond the veil lay the Most Holy Place, also called the Holy of Holies — the most sacred space in the Tabernacle. This inner chamber, a perfect cube measuring ten cubits on each side (about 15 feet), was the dwelling place of God's manifest presence among His people.

It was here that heaven touched earth. It was here that the glory of God rested above the Mercy Seat. And it is here that we learn what it means to truly encounter the presence of the Almighty.

### The Ark of the Covenant — God's Throne on Earth

The centerpiece of the Most Holy Place was the Ark of the Covenant (Exodus 25:10-22). Made of acacia wood and overlaid with pure gold, the Ark contained:

- The stone tablets of the Law

- A pot of manna

- Aaron's rod that budded

Above the Ark was the Mercy Seat, a solid gold cover with two cherubim facing each other, their wings outstretched, overshadowing the Ark.

This was no ordinary box. The Ark symbolized God's throne on earth — His covenant, His provision, His authority, and His mercy.

### The Shekinah Glory — God's Manifest Presence

Above the Mercy Seat dwelled the visible glory of God — the Shekinah. This radiant light represented God's immediate presence. It was the most sacred reality Israel knew, the ultimate fulfillment of God's promise:

"And let them make Me a sanctuary, that I may dwell among them" (Exodus 25:8).

The glory that once walked with Adam in the garden now rested above the Ark, hidden behind the veil, yet near to His people.

Brandon M. Crooker

### The Day of Atonement — The Way Into the Most Holy Place

Only once a year, on the Day of Atonement (Yom Kippur), could the High Priest enter the Most Holy Place (Leviticus 16). He came with the blood of sacrifice, sprinkled on and before the Mercy Seat, to atone for the sins of the nation.

This solemn ceremony taught that access to God's presence required atonement — the shedding of blood to cover sin. Without blood, there was no entry, no mercy, no fellowship.

### The Most Holy Place and Christ

The Most Holy Place pointed forward to Jesus Christ, our Great High Priest (Hebrews 9:11-12). Christ did not enter an earthly sanctuary with the blood of animals:

"But Christ came as High Priest... not with the blood of goats and calves, but with His own blood He entered the Most Holy Place once for all, having obtained eternal redemption" (Hebrews 9:11-12).

Through His sacrifice, Jesus secured for us access to the true Most Holy Place — the very throne of God in heaven.

The Ark points to Christ:

- The Law inside the Ark — Christ fulfilled the Law perfectly.
- The manna — Christ is the Bread of Life.
- The rod that budded — Christ is our resurrected High Priest.

The Mercy Seat represents the atoning work of Jesus, where mercy triumphs over judgment for all who believe.

### The Presence of God Today

Because of Christ's finished work, the Most Holy Place is no longer off-limits. We are invited to draw near:

"Therefore, brethren, having boldness to enter the Holiest by the blood of Jesus... let us draw near with a true heart in full assurance of faith" (Hebrews 10:19, 22).

God's presence is no longer confined to a tent or temple. By His Spirit, He dwells within every believer, making us temples of the living God (1 Corinthians 6:19).

## Reflection

The Most Holy Place teaches us the wonder of God's presence and the cost of access.

- Do you value the privilege of drawing near to God?

- Are you living in awe of His holiness and the mercy given through Christ?

- Is your heart a sanctuary where God's presence dwells richly?

The Most Holy Place calls us to worship, to reverence, and to joyful fellowship with the God who dwells with His people.

## Key Takeaway

The Most Holy Place reveals God's heart to dwell with His people — and through Christ, we are invited into His presence with boldness and awe.

# Chapter 7

# Christ, the Fulfillment of the Tabernacle

The Tabernacle was never meant to be the final destination in God's plan. It was a shadow, a type, a prophetic picture pointing to a greater reality — Jesus Christ. Every element of the Tabernacle, from its entrance gate to its innermost chamber, finds its fulfillment in Him.

When John wrote, "The Word became flesh and dwelt among us" (John 1:14), the word dwelt literally means tabernacled. In Christ, God Himself came to dwell among His people, not in a tent of animal skins, but in human flesh. The Tabernacle's deepest purpose was to prepare our understanding for the coming of the true and better Dwelling Place of God.

### Christ the Gate — The Only Way In

The Tabernacle had only one entrance. Likewise, Christ declared:

"I am the door. If anyone enters by Me, he will be saved" (John 10:9).

There is no other way to God. Just as the Israelites could not enter the Tabernacle except through the gate, so we cannot enter fellowship with God except through Jesus Christ.

### Christ the Altar — The Perfect Sacrifice

The Brazen Altar was the place of substitutionary death. Every offering pointed to the Lamb of God who would take away the sin of the world (John 1:29).

Jesus fulfilled the altar through His once-for-all sacrifice at Calvary:

"Christ also suffered once for sins, the just for the unjust, that He might bring us to God" (1 Peter 3:18).

No more need for continual sacrifices — Christ's offering was sufficient.

### Christ the Laver — The Cleansing Word

The Bronze Laver signified cleansing and sanctification. Jesus not only forgives sin but cleanses us from it:

"That He might sanctify and cleanse her with the washing of water by the word" (Ephesians 5:26).

Christ is both the One who purifies and the Word that purifies.

### Christ the Bread of Life

The Table of Showbread symbolized God's provision. Jesus said:

"I am the bread of life. He who comes to Me shall never hunger" (John 6:35).

Christ nourishes our souls, sustaining us with His presence and truth.

### Christ the Light of the World

The Golden Lampstand brought light to the Holy Place. Jesus declared:

"I am the light of the world. He who follows Me shall not walk in darkness, but have the light of life" (John 8:12).

He is our guide, our revelation, and the One who drives out darkness.

### Christ our Intercessor

The Altar of Incense pointed to continual prayer and intercession. Christ now lives to intercede for us:

"Therefore He is also able to save to the uttermost those who come to God through Him, since He always lives to make intercession for them" (Hebrews 7:25).

Our prayers are acceptable to God because of Jesus, our High Priest.

### Christ the Veil and the Way

The Veil was the barrier between God and man — until Christ. At His death, the veil was torn, signifying the new and living way He opened:

"By a new and living way which He consecrated for us, through the veil, that is, His flesh" (Hebrews 10:20).

Christ's body, torn for us, removed the separation and invites us into

God's presence.

## Christ our Mercy Seat

The Ark of the Covenant and Mercy Seat were the earthly throne of God's presence. Christ is now our mercy seat — our propitiation:

"And He Himself is the propitiation for our sins" (1 John 2:2).

In Him, mercy triumphs over judgment, and we find grace.

## The Tabernacle's True Fulfillment

Every element of the Tabernacle finds its meaning in Jesus. He is:

- The Way (Gate)
- The Sacrifice (Altar)
- The Sanctifier (Laver)
- The Sustainer (Bread)
- The Light (Lampstand)
- The Intercessor (Incense)
- The Access (Veil)
- The Mercy (Mercy Seat)

The earthly Tabernacle was temporary; Christ is eternal. The Tabernacle was a shadow; Christ is the substance.

## Reflection

The Tabernacle's design was always meant to point us to Jesus.

- Do you see Him in every part of God's redemptive plan?
- Are you daily relying on Christ as your access, provision, light, and mercy?

Let the shadow lead you to the substance — let the pattern lead you to the Person of Jesus Christ.

## Key Takeaway

The Tabernacle was God's picture book of salvation, and Christ is its perfect fulfillment. Through Him, we draw near to God.

# Chapter 8

# The High Priest and the Better Covenant

The Tabernacle was not just about sacred spaces and symbolic furniture — it was also about sacred service. At the heart of Tabernacle worship stood the High Priest, the one chosen to enter the Most Holy Place, to offer sacrifices, and to stand between God and His people. But even the greatest of Israel's High Priests pointed to a greater, eternal priesthood — that of Jesus Christ, the Mediator of a better covenant.

### The High Priest of the Old Covenant

Under the Old Covenant, the High Priest was the most important figure in Israel's religious life. Clothed in holy garments, bearing the names of the twelve tribes on his breastplate and shoulders, he represented the people before God.

His most solemn duty was on the Day of Atonement, when he entered the Most Holy Place with the blood of sacrifice to make atonement for the sins of the nation (Leviticus 16). He entered in fear and trembling, for he was a sinful man ministering before a holy God.

Yet, the work of the High Priest was:

- Limited — he could only enter once a year

- Temporary — his atonement had to be repeated annually

- Ineffective for the conscience — it covered sin but could not cleanse the heart (Hebrews 10:1-4)

The priesthood itself was imperfect, because it was carried out by men who shared in the sinfulness of those they represented.

### Jesus, Our Great High Priest

When Christ came, He fulfilled and surpassed everything the High Priest of Israel symbolized. The book of Hebrews declares:

"Seeing then that we have a great High Priest who has passed through the heavens, Jesus the Son of God, let us hold fast our confession" (Hebrews 4:14).

Whereas the earthly High Priest entered the earthly sanctuary, Christ entered the true sanctuary — heaven itself — offering His own blood for our redemption (Hebrews 9:11-12).

What makes Jesus the greater High Priest?

- He is sinless — unlike earthly priests, He had no sin of His own (Hebrews 7:26-27)

- He offered Himself — He was both Priest and Sacrifice (Hebrews 9:14)

- His atonement is once for all — never needing to be repeated (Hebrews 10:10-12)

- He intercedes continually — "He ever lives to make intercession for them" (Hebrews 7:25)

Christ's priesthood is superior because it is perfect, eternal, and effective to cleanse the conscience and transform the heart.

### The Better Covenant

The old priesthood was tied to the Old Covenant, a covenant based on the Law written on tablets of stone. It required repeated sacrifices and constant reminders of sin.

But in Christ, we have a better covenant:

"But now He has obtained a more excellent ministry, inasmuch as He is also Mediator of a better covenant, which was established on better promises" (Hebrews 8:6).

This better covenant:

- Is based on grace, not works

- Writes God's law on our hearts, not just on stone (Hebrews 8:10)

- Offers complete forgiveness — "Their sins and their lawless deeds I will remember no more" (Hebrews 8:12)

- Gives us direct access to God, without the need for earthly mediators

Through Christ, we have what the Tabernacle could only foreshadow — true fellowship with God, grounded in a perfect sacrifice and a living High Priest.

## Reflection

The priesthood and covenant of Christ are far better than the shadowy system of the Tabernacle.

- Are you trusting in your own efforts, or are you relying on Jesus, your Great High Priest?

- Do you approach God with confidence, knowing that Christ intercedes for you?

The Tabernacle priesthood was temporary. The priesthood of Christ is eternal. And through Him, we are welcomed into the presence of God.

## Key Takeaway

Jesus is the Great High Priest of a better covenant — one that offers complete forgiveness, direct access to God, and eternal salvation.

# Chapter 9

# Living Tabernacles — God in Us

The Tabernacle of Moses was a glorious symbol of God's desire to dwell among His people. But even as the Israelites gazed at its golden furnishings and marveled at the cloud of glory, the Tabernacle was never meant to be the final expression of God's presence.

The true purpose of the Tabernacle was to foreshadow a greater reality — a time when God would no longer dwell in a tent of skins or a temple of stone, but within His people themselves. Through Christ and the gift of the Holy Spirit, we have become living tabernacles, carrying the presence of God everywhere we go.

### God's Dwelling Place Is No Longer in Tents or Temples

The apostle Paul declared this profound truth:

"Do you not know that you are the temple of God and that the Spirit of God dwells in you?" (1 Corinthians 3:16)

No longer is God's presence confined behind curtains or hidden in a sacred room. The veil has been torn, and God's Spirit now resides within every believer. We are His sanctuary, His dwelling, His tabernacle on earth.

Whereas the Israelites had to journey to the Tabernacle or the Temple to encounter God, we now carry His presence with us — in our hearts, in our lives, in our very beings.

### The Indwelling Spirit: A Fulfillment of the Tabernacle's Purpose

The Tabernacle taught Israel about holiness, sacrifice, prayer, and worship — but these things were external. The Holy Spirit takes what was external and makes it internal.

Through the Spirit:

- The law is written on our hearts (Hebrews 8:10)

- We become the dwelling place of God (Ephesians 2:22)

- We offer spiritual sacrifices — our lives, our praise, our service (1 Peter 2:5)

Whereas the Tabernacle was a shadow, the Spirit's indwelling is the substance. God no longer dwells near His people; He dwells within His people.

## The Call to Holiness

Just as the Tabernacle was to be kept pure and consecrated, so we are called to live holy lives:

"Or do you not know that your body is the temple of the Holy Spirit who is in you... therefore glorify God in your body and in your spirit, which are God's" (1 Corinthians 6:19-20).

Being a living tabernacle means our lives should reflect the glory and character of the God who dwells within. We are to be set apart, vessels of honor, carrying His presence into a world in need.

## A Life of Continual Worship

The priests of the Tabernacle ministered daily — tending the lamp, offering incense, placing the bread — all in service to God. As living tabernacles, our lives should be marked by:

- Continual worship — not limited to a location or event
- Prayer without ceasing — our incense rising daily
- The light of Christ shining through us — as the lampstand burned continually

Our whole lives become an act of worship, because God dwells within.

## Reflection

The Tabernacle was glorious, but its true glory was in pointing forward to the indwelling Spirit.

- Are you aware that you carry God's presence wherever you go?
- Does your life reflect the holiness and beauty of the One who lives within you?

- Are you offering yourself daily as a living sacrifice, bringing glory to God?

The Tabernacle journey leads us to this truth: we are now God's dwelling place, called to live for His glory.

## Key Takeaway

The ultimate purpose of the Tabernacle was fulfilled in Christ and the Holy Spirit — making us living tabernacles where God's presence dwells and His glory shines.

# *Chapter 10*

# *Worship According to the Pattern*

The Tabernacle was not just a tent in the wilderness; it was a divine blueprint for worship. God gave Moses precise instructions, saying:

"According to all that I show you, that is, the pattern of the tabernacle and the pattern of all its furnishings, just so you shall make it" (Exodus 25:9).

This wasn't because God was concerned with aesthetics or ritual for ritual's sake. The pattern of the Tabernacle revealed the heart of worship — that true worship must be according to God's design, not our preferences.

As believers today, the Tabernacle reminds us that worship is not about what pleases us, but about what pleases the One we worship.

### God's Pattern Requires Reverence

The Tabernacle's details — from the materials used to the sequence of approach — all emphasized God's holiness. The closer one moved toward the Most Holy Place, the greater the requirements for purity, sacrifice, and sanctification.

This teaches us that worship is not casual. While Christ has opened the way for us to boldly enter God's presence, we must still come with reverence and awe:

"Let us have grace, by which we may serve God acceptably with reverence and godly fear. For our God is a consuming fire" (Hebrews 12:28-29).

True worship acknowledges the greatness and holiness of the God we approach.

### God's Pattern Centers on Sacrifice

In the Tabernacle, worship began at the altar. There could be no fellowship without the shedding of blood. Worship was costly. It required the offering of what was precious.

Today, we come to God not with the blood of animals, but through the perfect sacrifice of Jesus Christ (Hebrews 10:19-22). And we are called to present ourselves as living sacrifices:

"I beseech you therefore, brethren, by the mercies of God, that you present your bodies a living sacrifice, holy, acceptable to God, which is your reasonable service" (Romans 12:1).

God's pattern for worship always involves surrender.

### God's Pattern Involves Continual Devotion

The priests' duties were daily, not just on special occasions:

- The lampstand was kept burning

- Incense was offered morning and evening

- The bread of the Presence was always before the Lord

Worship is not an event. It's a lifestyle — a continual offering of ourselves, our praise, and our prayers to God. As Paul wrote:

"Pray without ceasing" (1 Thessalonians 5:17).

Our lives are to be marked by ongoing communion with God.

### Worship in Spirit and in Truth

Jesus told the woman at the well:

"But the hour is coming, and now is, when the true worshipers will worship the Father in spirit and truth; for the Father is seeking such to worship Him" (John 4:23).

The Tabernacle pattern teaches us truth — God's way of approach through sacrifice, cleansing, and reverence. The Spirit enables us to live out that truth, making our worship genuine, alive, and God-glorifying.

Worship according to the pattern means worship that aligns with God's revelation (truth) and is empowered by God's Spirit.

### Reflection

The Tabernacle teaches us that God cares how He is worshiped.

- Are we worshiping in spirit and in truth, according to God's Word?

- Is our worship marked by reverence, sacrifice, and continual devotion?

- Are we living lives that glorify the God who dwells within us?

Let us build our worship on God's pattern, not our own, that He may be honored in all we do.

## Key Takeaway

Worship according to the pattern is worship that honors God's holiness, relies on Christ's sacrifice, and offers our lives as continual devotion in spirit and truth.

# Chapter 11

# Journey Through the Tabernacle — A Model of Spiritual Growth

The Tabernacle was more than a structure; it was a spiritual journey. Each step deeper into the Tabernacle revealed more about God's nature and taught God's people how to draw near to Him. This journey from the Outer Court to the Most Holy Place mirrors the believer's own walk of spiritual growth and intimacy with God.

The Tabernacle shows us that coming close to God is a progressive journey — one of salvation, cleansing, devotion, and communion.

*Step 1: The Gate — Entering Through Christ*

The first step is through the gate of the Outer Court — the one and only entrance. This gate represents Christ, the only way to the Father:

"I am the way, the truth, and the life. No one comes to the Father except through Me" (John 14:6).

Spiritual growth begins with salvation — acknowledging that Christ is the only door to God.

*Step 2: The Brazen Altar — The Cross of Sacrifice*

Next, we come to the Brazen Altar, where the blood of sacrifice was shed. This altar points to the cross of Christ, where our sins were atoned for:

"Without shedding of blood there is no remission" (Hebrews 9:22).

Here, we learn forgiveness. True spiritual growth starts when we recognize the cost of our salvation and live in gratitude for the Lamb who was slain.

*Step 3: The Laver — Cleansing and Sanctification*

At the Bronze Laver, the priests washed their hands and feet before ministering. For us, this symbolizes sanctification — the ongoing work of the Word and Spirit cleansing our lives:

"That He might sanctify and cleanse her with the washing of water by the word" (Ephesians 5:26).

Spiritual growth requires daily cleansing — a life submitted to the purifying work of God.

*Step 4: The Holy Place — The Life of Devotion*

Entering the Holy Place, we encounter:

- The Table of Showbread — fellowship with Christ, the Bread of Life

- The Lampstand — guidance and illumination by the Holy Spirit

- The Altar of Incense — a life marked by prayer and intercession

Here, we learn devotion. Spiritual maturity deepens as we feed on God's Word, walk in the Spirit's light, and maintain constant communion through prayer.

*Step 5: The Veil — Access Opened*

The veil that once barred access to the Most Holy Place was torn at Christ's death. Spiritual growth moves us from seeing God as distant to knowing Him as near, through the torn veil of Christ's body (Hebrews 10:19-20).

*Step 6: The Most Holy Place — Communion with God*

At last, the journey brings us to the Most Holy Place, where God's presence dwelt above the Mercy Seat. This is where spiritual growth finds its goal: intimate communion with God.

The believer who journeys through the Tabernacle pattern learns to live not in the Outer Court of distant faith, but in the Most Holy Place of daily fellowship with the living God.

**A Daily Journey**

While this journey reflects stages of spiritual growth, it is also a daily path. Every day, we:

- Enter through Christ

- Thank Him for His sacrifice

- Submit to His cleansing

- Feed on His Word

- Walk in His light

- Pray continually

- Draw near to His presence

Spiritual growth is not a destination but a lifelong pilgrimage into the heart of God.

## Reflection

The Tabernacle invites you on a journey of transformation.

- Where are you on this spiritual path today?

- Are you lingering at the gate, or are you pressing deeper into God's presence?

- Are you allowing Christ's sacrifice, God's Word, and the Spirit's light to shape your daily walk?

The call is clear: Come closer. Journey deeper. Grow in grace.

## Key Takeaway

The journey through the Tabernacle models our spiritual growth — from salvation at the gate to communion with God in the Most Holy Place. Every step draws us nearer to Him.

# Chapter 12

# The Tabernacle and the Church

The Tabernacle was God's dwelling place among His people in the wilderness, but its deeper purpose was to reveal timeless truths about His presence, His people, and His plan. As we look at the church today — the Body of Christ — we can see how the pattern of the Tabernacle still speaks.

The church is called to be a dwelling place of God (Ephesians 2:22), a holy community where His presence is manifest, His name is glorified, and His mission is carried out. The Tabernacle offers vital lessons for how we, as the church, are to live and worship together.

## The Church as God's Dwelling

In the wilderness, God's glory rested above the Mercy Seat. Today, His glory is meant to be seen in His people:

"In whom you also are being built together for a dwelling place of God in the Spirit" (Ephesians 2:22).

The Tabernacle was portable — God's presence journeyed with His people. Likewise, the church is not confined to buildings or locations. Wherever believers gather in Christ's name, God is there (Matthew 18:20).

## Unity: One Tabernacle, One Body

The Tabernacle was one structure with many parts, all working together according to God's pattern. In the same way, the church is one body with many members:

"For we, though many, are one bread and one body; for we all partake of that one bread" (1 Corinthians 10:17).

Just as every piece of the Tabernacle had its purpose, so every believer has a role in the church. Unity is not sameness — it is diverse parts working together under God's design.

## The Call to Holiness

The Tabernacle was holy because God dwelt there. Everything associated with it was set apart for His glory. So too the church is called to holiness:

"But as He who called you is holy, you also be holy in all your conduct" (1 Peter 1:15).

The church must reflect the character of the God who dwells within. We are to be a people marked by purity, love, humility, and truth.

## Worship and Mission

The Tabernacle existed for God's glory — a place of worship where sacrifices were offered, prayers were raised, and God's name was exalted. The church exists for the same purpose:

"That you may proclaim the praises of Him who called you out of darkness into His marvelous light" (1 Peter 2:9).

But the church's mission extends beyond the camp. The Tabernacle was at the center of Israel's camp — visible to all, a witness to the nations. The church is to be a city set on a hill, declaring the good news of Jesus to a watching world (Matthew 5:14-16).

## The Glory of God Among His People

In the Tabernacle, the visible glory of God filled the sanctuary (Exodus 40:34-35). In the church, His glory is to be seen not in a cloud or fire, but in transformed lives:

"Christ in you, the hope of glory" (Colossians 1:27).

When the church lives according to God's pattern — in unity, holiness, and love — His glory is revealed through us.

## Reflection

The Tabernacle provides a powerful picture of what the church is called to be.

- Are we living as God's dwelling place, where His presence is known and honored?

- Are we united, working together as one body for His purposes?

- Are we proclaiming His glory, both in worship and in our

witness to the world?

The Tabernacle calls us to be a people where God's presence dwells, where His glory shines, and where His mission is fulfilled.

## Key Takeaway

The church is the living Tabernacle of God today — called to unity, holiness, worship, and mission, that His glory may be seen among all nations.

# Study Questions

## *Chapter 1: God's Desire to Dwell Among His People*

1. What does the Tabernacle reveal about God's desire for relationship with His people?

2. How does Exodus 25:8 shape our understanding of God's purpose for the Tabernacle?

3. In what ways does the Tabernacle reflect God's plan to restore fellowship with humanity?

4. How can we apply the truth of God's desire to dwell among us to our daily lives?

## *Chapter 2: The Pattern Shown on the Mount*

1. Why was it important for Moses to follow the exact pattern shown on the mountain?

2. How does the Tabernacle reflect heavenly realities (Hebrews 8:5)?

3. What lessons does the precision of God's instructions teach us about worship and obedience?

4. How can we ensure our worship aligns with God's revealed pattern today?

## *Chapter 3: The Outer Court — A Place of Access*

1. What is the significance of there being only one gate into the Tabernacle court?

2. How does the Brazen Altar point to Christ's sacrifice?

3. What does the Bronze Laver teach us about cleansing and sanctification?

4. How does the progression through the Outer Court illustrate the beginning of our spiritual journey?

### *Chapter 4: The Holy Place — The Life of Devotion*

1. What spiritual truths are symbolized by the Table of Showbread, the Golden Lampstand, and the Altar of Incense?

2. How do these furnishings speak to a believer's daily walk with God?

3. What role does prayer (represented by the Altar of Incense) play in spiritual growth?

4. How can you cultivate continual devotion in your own life?

### *Chapter 5: The Veil — Separation and Invitation*

1. What did the veil represent under the Old Covenant?

2. How did the tearing of the veil at Christ's death change our access to God?

3. What does the veil teach us about God's holiness and our need for atonement?

4. How does Christ's work invite us into deeper fellowship with God?

### *Chapter 6: The Most Holy Place — The Presence of God*

1. What was the significance of the Ark of the Covenant and the Mercy Seat?

2. How did the Day of Atonement point to the work of Christ?

3. What does it mean to live in God's presence today?

4. How can we cultivate a greater awareness of God's presence in

our daily lives?

### *Chapter 7: Christ, the Fulfillment of the Tabernacle*

1. How does each element of the Tabernacle point to Jesus Christ?

2. What does it mean for Christ to be our sacrifice, our bread, our light, and our access?

3. How does understanding the Tabernacle enhance our appreciation for Christ's work?

4. In what ways can we daily rely on Christ as our true Tabernacle?

### *Chapter 8: The High Priest and the Better Covenant*

1. How was Christ's priesthood superior to that of the Old Covenant High Priest?

2. What makes the New Covenant better than the Old Covenant?

3. How does Jesus' role as our High Priest impact your prayer life?

4. What does it mean to live under the better covenant today?

### *Chapter 9: Living Tabernacles — God in Us*

1. What does it mean that believers are now God's dwelling place?

2. How should the reality of God living within us affect how we live and worship?

3. In what ways can your life reflect the holiness of the One who dwells in you?

4. How does the concept of being a living tabernacle challenge

your daily walk?

## *Chapter 10: Worship According to the Pattern*

1. Why does God care about the pattern of worship?

2. How do sacrifice, reverence, and continual devotion shape true worship?

3. What does it mean to worship in spirit and truth?

4. How can we align our worship today with God's revealed pattern?

## *Chapter 11: Journey Through the Tabernacle — A Model of Spiritual Growth*

1. How does the journey through the Tabernacle mirror the believer's spiritual growth?

2. What are the stages of spiritual growth symbolized in the Tabernacle?

3. Where do you see yourself on this spiritual journey?

4. How can you press deeper into communion with God?

## *Chapter 12: The Tabernacle and the Church*

1. How is the church today called to reflect the truths of the Tabernacle?

2. What does it mean for the church to be God's dwelling place?

3. How can the church pursue unity, holiness, and mission in light of the Tabernacle?

4. In what ways can your local church better reflect the glory of God?

# OTHER BOOKS BY BY BRANDON M. CROOKER:

FAITH TO FAITH: WHAT IS FAITH? WHERE DOES IT COME
FROM? AND HOW DO WE USE IT?
ISBN: 979-8549234253

MATTERS OF THE HEART: EXPLORING WHAT THE BIBLE
SAYS ABOUT THE HEART
ISBN: 979-8475781692

RESTORE: A BIBLICAL GUIDE TO RESTORATION &
RECONCILIATION
ISBN: 979-8443107134

TRAIL BLAZERS: FORGING PATHS OF FAITH, COURAGE
AND KINGDOM LEGACY
ISBN: 979-8285366157

UPROOTING DOUBT: RESTORING SPIRITUAL
EQUILIBRIUM
ISBN: 979-8769137945

SPEAK LORD THY SERVANT HEARETH: LEARNING TO BE
SENSITIVE TO THE VOICE OF GOD
ISBN: 979-8768670528

THE EPIDEMIC OF FEAR: 2020
ISBN: 979-8284336694

HOPE AFTER FAILURE
ISBN: 979-8375199030

HEAVEN'S MANDATE: WALKING IN DIVINE AUTHORITY
ISBN: 979-8287617240

THE MESSAGE OF SALVATION
ISBN: 979-8396368927

TONGUES: THE LANGUAGE OF THE SPIRIT
ISBN: 979-8288364839

THE VOICE OF THE PROPHET
ISBN: 979-8394927034

WEAPONS & WARFARE: A COLLECTION OF SERMONS
ISBN: 979-8494729217

Visit the author's website at:
WWW.BRANDONMCROOKER.COM

www.ingramcontent.com/pod-product-compliance
Lightning Source LLC
Chambersburg PA
CBHW072023060426
42449CB00034B/2059